How to use this book

Follow the advice, in italics, where given.
Support the children as they read the text that is shaded in cream.
***Praise** the children at every step!*
Detailed guidance is provided in the Read Write Inc. Phonics Handbook.
Activity 8 (Answer the 'questions to read and answer') only appears in Sets 4–7.

8 reading activities

Children:

1 *Practise reading the speed sounds.*
2 *Read the green and red words for the non-fiction text.*
3 *Listen as you read the introduction.*
4 *Discuss the vocabulary check with you.*
5 *Read the non-fiction text.*
6 *Re-read the non-fiction text and discuss the 'questions to talk about'.*
7 *Re-read the non-fiction text with fluency and expression.*
9 *Practise reading the speed words.*

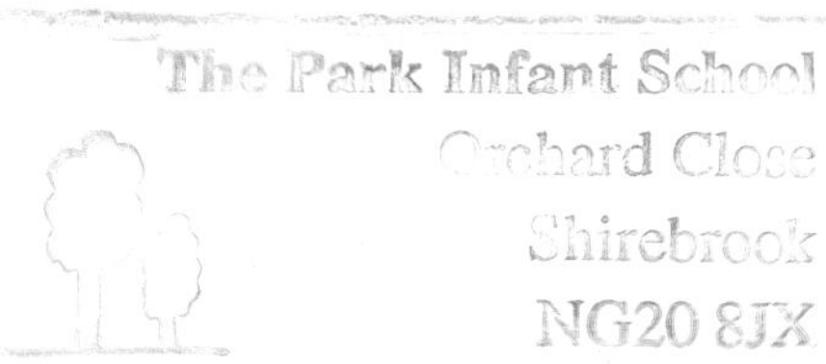

Speed sounds

Consonants *Say the pure sounds (do not add 'uh').*

f ff	l **ll** (circled)	m mm	n nn kn	r rr	s **ss** (circled)	v ve	z zz s	sh	th	ng nk

b bb	c k ck	d dd	g gg	h	j	p pp	qu	t tt	w wh	x	y	ch tch

Vowels *Say the vowel sound and then the word, e.g. 'a', 'at'.*

at	hen head	in	on	up	day	see happy	high	blow

zoo	look	car	for	fair	whirl	shout	boy

Each box contains one sound but sometimes more than one grapheme. Focus graphemes are ***circled****.*

Green words

Read in Fred Talk (pure sounds).

Jay	way	clay	lays	tray	stays
lump	off	next			

Read in syllables.

bott` om → bottom

Read the root word first and then with the ending.

add → adds	press → presses	lay → lays
stay → stays	roll → rolls	

Red words

he the of so

tall er* makes* making*

red for this book only

Jay's clay pot

Introduction

Have you ever made a pot at school? In this book you will see Jay making a pot. He uses a special material called clay. Clay starts off soft and then when you have finished shaping it, you can put it in a special oven and it goes hard.

Written by Gill Munton

Vocabulary check

Discuss the meaning (as used in the non-fiction text) after the children have read the word.

	definition
clay	*sticky mud that you can make things with*

Punctuation to note:

Jay	Capital letters for names
This He	Capital letters that start sentences
.	Full stop at the end of each sentence
,	Comma to show a pause
!	Exclamation mark

Jay is making a clay pot.

He lays a lump of clay on a tray.

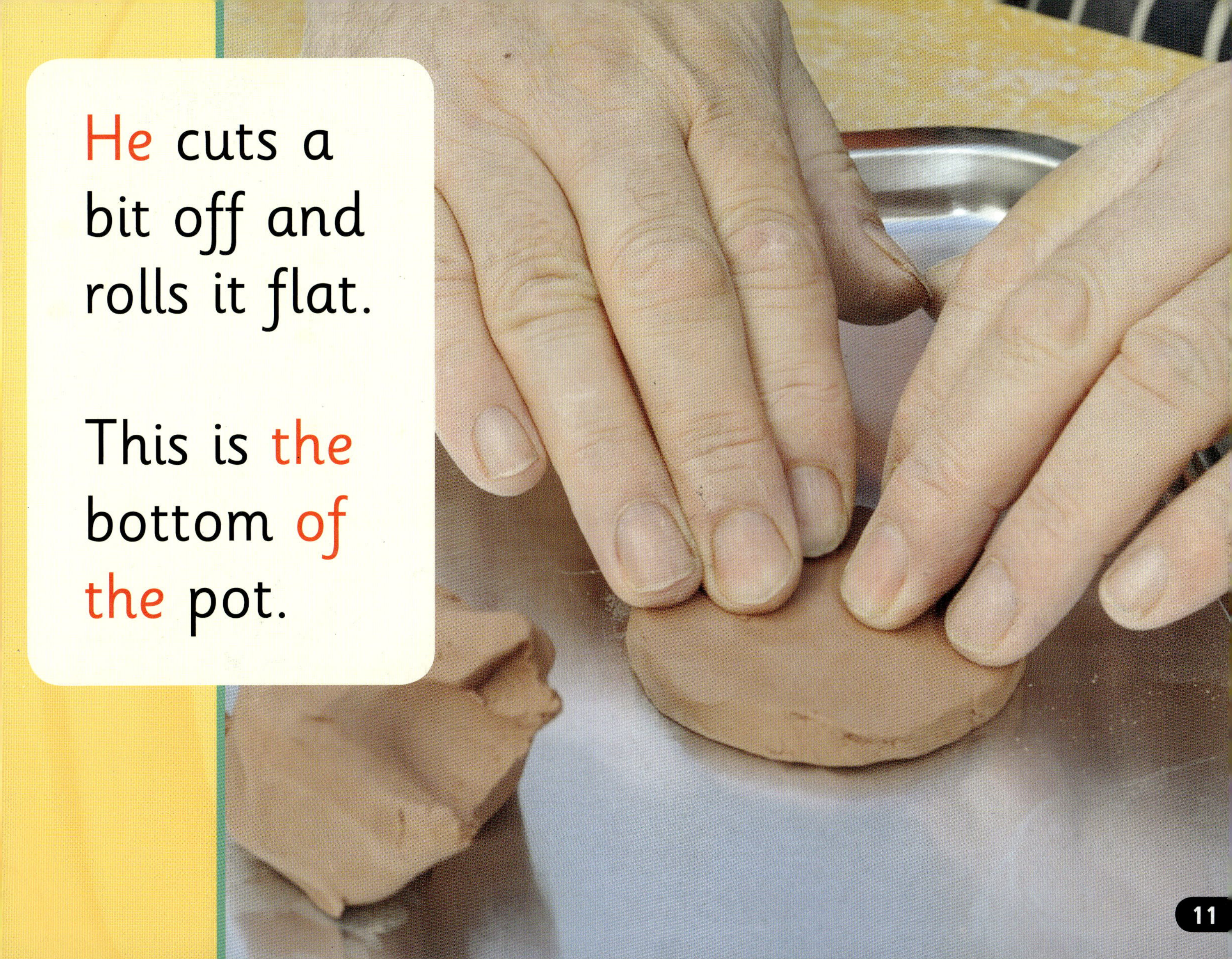

He cuts a bit off and rolls it flat.

This is the bottom of the pot.

Next, Jay rolls up the rest of the clay.

He cuts a bit off and makes a ring.

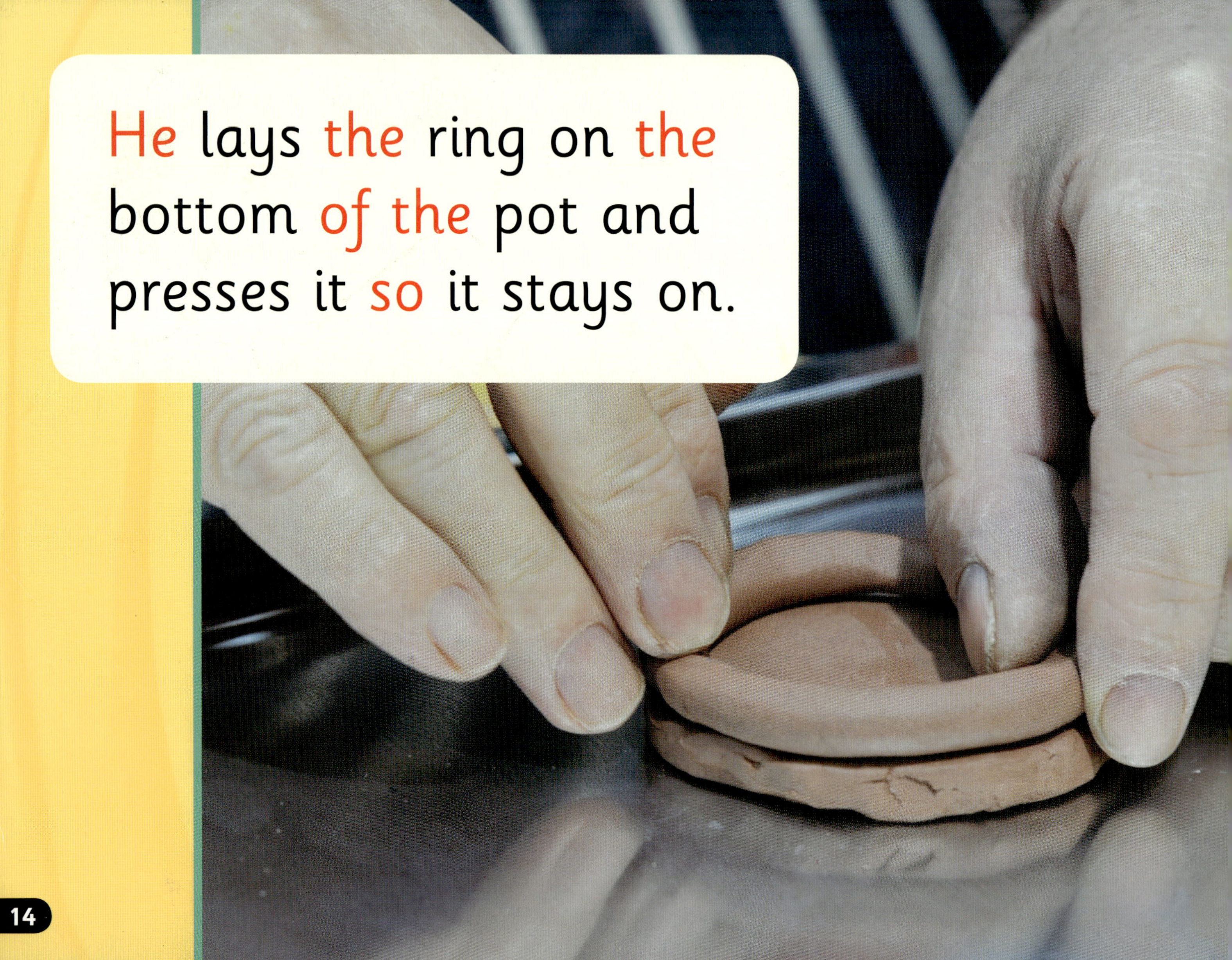

He lays the ring on the bottom of the pot and presses it so it stays on.

Then he adds the next ring, and the next.

In this way, the pot gets taller.

Jay puts big spots on it with a brush!

Questions to talk about 

Re-read the page. Read the question to the children. Tell them whether it is a FIND IT *question or* PROVE IT *question.*

FIND IT	**PROVE IT**
✓ *Turn to the page*	✓ *Turn to the page*
✓ *Read the question*	✓ *Read the question*
✓ *Find the answer*	✓ *Find your evidence*
	✓ *Explain why*

Page 11:	FIND IT	*What does Jay do to make the flat piece for the bottom of the pot?*
Page 13:	FIND IT	*What shape does Jay make with the clay?*
Page 14:	FIND IT	*What does Jay do to make the ring stick to the bottom of the pot?*
Page 16:	FIND IT	*What does Jay use to decorate the pot?*

Speed words

Children practise reading the words across the rows, down the columns and in and out of order clearly and quickly.

way	rolls	pot	press	adds
next	off	clay	spot	rest
lump	tray	bottom	and	puts
gets	ring	cut	bit	lay